THE LITTLE BOOK OF
ODDLY SPECIFIC POETRY

THE
LITTLE
BOOK
OF

oddly
specific
poetry.

WILL BECKER

Published by Elemental Words Press
Colorado, USA

Cover and text design: KP Books

ISBN: 979-8-218-53461-5

CONTENTS

CONTENTS

CONTENTS

CONTENTS

CONTENTS

INTRODUCTION

More often than I would like to admit, I am overwhelmed by the plethora of things that I could do creatively, if only time and attention were limitless. Perplexed by a growing buffet of options, I either exhaust myself by trying too much and getting burned out—or I am paralyzed by a sea of possibilities and choose none.

In pursuit of a good mental challenge, I leaned on two unique word-play structures you'll discover here in *Oddly Specific Poetry*. These formats give a creative constraint to work within that provides both focus and fun.

It turns out that I am not the only one who enjoys this type of creative writing. Some writers choose to use a phonetic constraint, such as rhyme or syllables, while others may choose a visual constraint, such as patterns of words or letters. In the field of poetry, the advent of concrete poetry, or visual poetry, emphasizes the visual arrangement of words on the page.

You are probably familiar with syllabic verse, which is a poetic form that uses a constrained number of syllables for each line. Haiku is one of the better-known versions of this approach, using a pattern of 5, then 7, then 5 syllables. As much as I enjoy a good Haiku, I found that 3, then another 3, then 4 syllables provided an equally appealing structure. This inspired the "3/3/4" poem structure collection I've shared here.

Something interesting happened one day when I wrote a simple little play on words onto a Post-it note. I realized that it looked tidy and orderly. I wrote, I Am Not That Stuck. Noticing that each subsequent word had one more letter than the previous word, I arranged it vertically and proceeded to explore this approach as a poetic constraint. This led to my collection of "Pyramid Poems," as they look roughly like a triangle when viewed on a page.

Using the constraint of a set number of letters or syllables helps me to focus on the quality and specificity of each word. I wrote these poems for my own entertainment and edification. What I found, however, is that they provide a structure that I have not seen elsewhere. With that in mind, I offer this book as a contribution to the field of concrete and visual poetry. It is my hope that the "3/3/4 Syllable Poems" and "Pyramid Poems" might inspire others who are seeking a new structure for creative wordplay.

3/3/4 POEMS

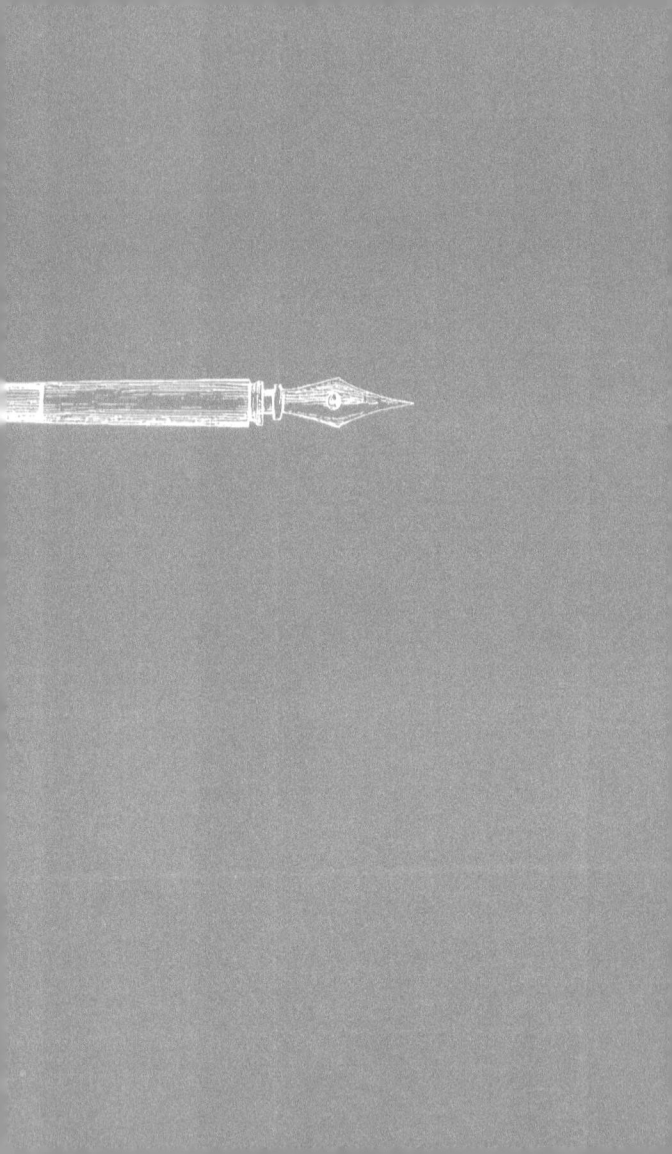

WHAT ARE
"3/3/4" POEMS?

When a poem is constrained by syllables, there is a phonetic rhythm to the experience of reading it. Like the Haiku or a good limerick, the reader begins to anticipate what will come next. Over time, I came to enjoy a different pattern: These poems have 3 syllables on line one, 3 syllables on line two, and 4 syllables on line three.

Plebeian

Poetry

Of the people.

Maybe I
Can write more
Insightfully.

I tried it
On a bad day,
Unfortunately.

Thin ice cracks.
I fall in
to disaster.

Getting old,
Working out,
Ibuprofin.

Zip lines go
Woosh, woosh, woosh.
Oh my goodness.

I traveled.

You traveled.

We traveled not.

I like you.
You like me.
That is not all.

Our Journey:

Adventure.

To where, we ask.

My Dad is
Far more cool
Than I will be.

Your laughter
Is my joy.
It's contagious.

When she cries,
Every tear
Falls down my cheek.

I am wont
To be near
Your happiness.

I miss you
Every day
Without you near.

Take my heart.
With you near,
I don't need it.

Politics

Division

Help the children.

Orgasm
Can make an
Organism.

I love her,
All of her,
I tell myself.

She flipped out.

I shut down.

It's not healthy.

Syllable
Syllable
Go to bed now.

Why Can't I
Go to sleep
Like my dog does?

I can't sleep,
So I think
About my life.

Should I try?
Should I not?
Paralysis.

Sometimes I
Need just me.
Isolation.

I win when
You go broke.
Monopoly.

Markets go
Up and down.
People react.

Please go far
From my door.
Solicitor.

I can do
What I want.
Autonomy.

Everything

Worrying

You are to me.

I love it.
I loathe it.
Information.

People help.
People try.
Appreciate.

The past is
What it was.
Now to forgive.

Feel the pain.

Let it hurt.

Progress slowly.

Hard work, and
hot day, and
cold, tasty drink.

Gardening.
Nourishment.
Planting my meals.

Tempers flare.

I go red.

Time Out For All.

I feel like

we met a

Lifetime ago.

A little
more today.
Accumulate.

Oh, what will
come to me?
Anticipate.

Trust that I
really do
love all of you.

Do what I
say and want.
Authority.

We vote for
folks that vote.
Democracy.

Don't want to,
but okay.
Obligation.

One day we
find we have
mortality.

You want it.

Not giving.

Opposition.

Could be right;
Could be wrong.
Our convictions.

Do it now.

Also, that.

Overwhelming.

Many things
still not done.
Multitasking.

Thought I knew
the best way.
Erroneous.

Surrendered.
And plundered.
Board game defeat.

I am not
always right.
Humility.

I go out
of my mind.
My quarantine.

I am not
as bad as
I feared I was.

I am not
as good as
I want to be.

I draw on
the margins
around us all.

A rage sowed.

A sewed rag.

A ragged sew.

I made some
bad mistakes.
Don't cancel me.

Speech is free,
but hatred
is expensive.

Your words hurt.

My pain heals.

Don't use bullets.

PYRAMID POEMS

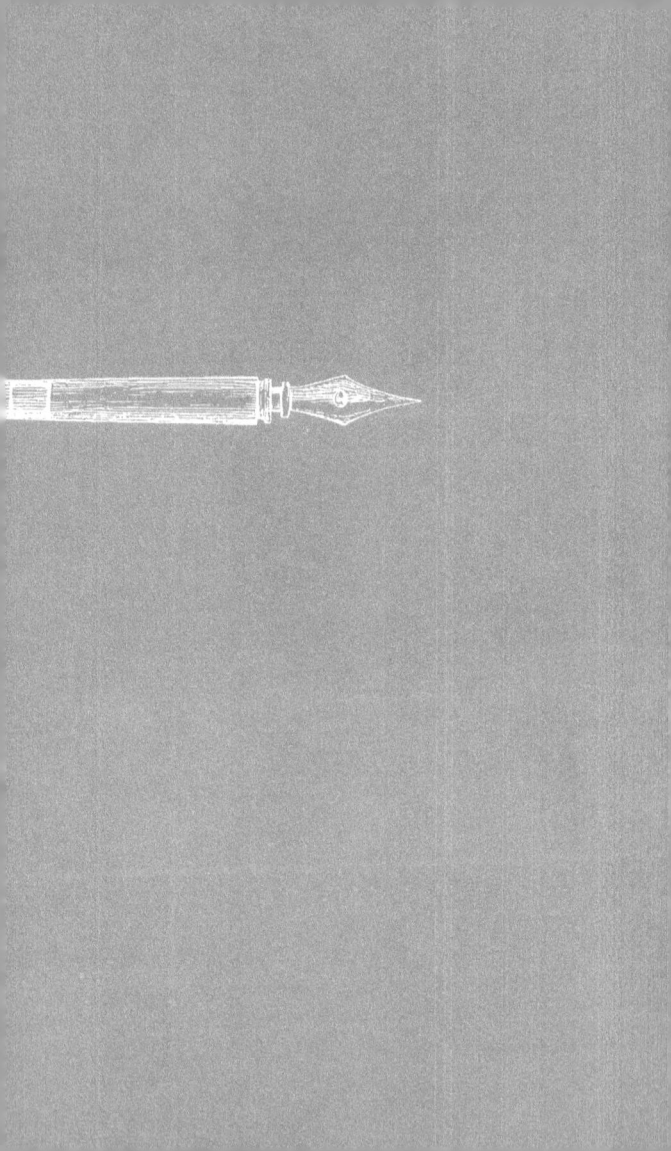

WHAT IS A
"PYRAMID POEM"?

A "Pyramid Poem" is a type of visual poetry in which each following line has one more letter (or one less) than the line before. This creates the shape of a pyramid of sorts on the page. These poems are naturally limited by the number of lines per page.

This type of poem provides a visual guide instead of a phonetic guide. The reader—and the writer—know that the words get longer (or shorter) with each line.

This format came by accident one day as I was trying to talk my way out of writer's block. I wrote down the words, *I Am Not That Stuck*. When I arranged it vertically, this opened a new way of looking at writing. What if my writing could be visually inspired? This led to the following collection of "Pyramid Poems."

I
Am
Not
That
Stuck.

I
Go
For
Iffy
Hopes.

I
Do
Act
Well
Among
Casual
Friends.

If
You
Only
Loved
Your
Own
Id.

Id is a concept developed by Sigmund Freud that represents the unconscious, primitive, impulsive, and instinctual part of the mind.

Id
Has
Will
Power
Beaten.

Ah,
One
More
Thing.
Always.

As
You
Said,
Grace,
Virtue,
Desires,
Overwhelm
Convention.

At

One

Time,

They'd

Suffer

Further.

Be

One

Many

Times.

It
Was
Lost
Until
Monday
Laundry.

My

Axe

Fell.

Ouchy.

I'm
Dad.
Live
Child,
Always.

I'm

Not

Very

Tired

This

Eve.

Zz.

If
The
Door
Opens,
Chance
Returns.

Love

Heart

Desire

Passion

Generous

Protector

Romantic

Feeling

Warmth

Proud

Hugs

Midnight
Carries
Weight.
Tired
Open
Eye.

Be
The
Only
Saver
Needed.

Go

Try

More

Crazy

Things.

Go
Buy
Less
Stuff
Than
You
Do.

I
Am
Yin &
Yang.

Yin,

Yang.

Roads

Zigzag

Towards

Generous

Abundance.

Fair
Minds,
Enough
Warning;
Actively
Skeptical.

Is

She

Love

After

Tumult?

Love

Has

Me.

My,

Has

Love

Grown

Beyond

Wildest

Dreams.

My,
How
Fate
Plays
Tricks.

My,

Was

That

Crazy.

So,

Was

That

Crazy

Insane?

Do

Any

Foes

Fight

Harder?

Do

Say

More.

To

All

That

Try

Me.

Battle

Rages

Into

You.

My

Luv

Won't

Curry

Favors,

Despite

Attempts.

Say
They
Loved
Beyond
Their
Day.

Fume.

Fumer.

Fuming.

Welcome,

Doghouse.

Lit.

Lite.

Light.

Little.

Literal.

Literacy.

Words

Fail

Now,

Me.

My

Cup

Full,

Tries,

Spills,

Runneth

Beyond

Limit.

Wait;

Worse

Crisis

Comes

Soon.

Tears
Edge
Near
For
Me.

Many

folks

toiled

against

memories.

Go
and
make
lives
better.

ABOUT THE AUTHOR

Will Becker grew up in the rural Napa Valley of Northern California, then went on to earn undergraduate and graduate degrees in Anthropology. After completing his Master's Thesis exploring the causes of the collapse of civilizations in the Early Bronze Age Northern Mesopotamia, he decided to work on more current issues. For close to a decade, he helped people start and grow nonprofit organizations. After that, he operated job training and environmental programs at a local Conservation Corps, including launching a Certified Organic Farm. After a sabbatical from the working world to be a stay-at-home father, he turned professional on one of the activities that he had long pursued personally—investing. He currently provides financial advice and spends his time with family and friends in the great outdoors.